Sarah and Paul
Go to the Museum

Discover About
The Ten Commandments

Derek Prime

Christian Focus Publications

© Derek Prime
ISBN 1 871676 37 3

Published by
Christian Focus Publications Ltd., Geanies House,
Fearn, Ross-shire, IV20 1TW, Scotland
website: http://www.christianfocus.org.uk

1st edition 1989
2nd edition 1995
3rd edition 1998
4th edition 2000

Cover design by Donna Macleod
Cover illustration by Andrew Tudor, Allied Artists
Black and white illustrations by Janis Mennie

Printed and bound in Great Britain by Cox & Wyman,
Reading.

CONTENTS

To Anna, Emily, Deborah, Andrew and Paul

1   A Rainy Afternoon

'That was a marvellous dinner!' exclaimed Mr MacDonald, as he folded up his napkin.

'It's left a lot of dishwashing, though,' answered Mrs MacDonald, frowning. 'Still I expect the twins will help me, won't you?'

'We'll lend a hand,' he replied. 'If the rain holds off, we'll go out for our usual walk. But I don't like the look of those dark clouds.'

'It's a pity when the weather's wet or rough on Sundays, isn't it, Dad?' asked Sarah.

'Why, because of our afternoon walk?'

'No, not only because of that.   I was thinking of how difficult you said it makes it for older people to get to church sometimes.'

'Yes,' agreed the twins' father.   'Still it's surprising how they manage.   They put some of the younger people to shame.   Now, what about that dishwashing?'

Sarah and Paul groaned and screwed up their noses in disgust.

'Do we have to?'

'If you really want to please me,' Mrs MacDonald called out from the kitchen.

'I wanted to read my library book,' complained Sarah.

'If you won't do it to please Mum, then I must tell you to do it because I say so,' said Mr MacDonald.

Sarah and Paul looked at one another and guessed what the other was thinking - Dad meant them to obey him.

The kitchen draining board was covered with plates and cooking utensils waiting to be dried, and some of the messier things still had to be washed.

'It won't take long, twins,' said Mrs MacDonald.

Paul took two plates to dry at once, because he had seen his father dry them like that. 'I can dry two plates together, Sarah.'

'No, you can't,' said his mother. 'You'll drop one.'

'I won't,' promised Paul. But no sooner had he said this than crash - a plate had fallen to the floor and had broken.

'There goes your pocket money for next week,' warned Mr MacDonald.

Paul looked at Sarah with a grim kind of smile. 'Everything happens to me.'

'Poor thing,' answered his mother with a laugh, when she saw how sorry he looked. 'Oh, look out of the window; it's pouring with rain.'

'No walk then this afternoon,' exclaimed Sarah. 'Will you play with us, Dad?'

'I'll see,' Mr MacDonald replied. 'But tell me first what you've been doing in Sunday School.'

'Learning the Ten Commandments.'

'Have you both learned them?'

'Yes,' said Sarah.

'All right, then; while we finish the dishes and put the things away, let me ask you some questions!'

'Can we take it in turns, Dad?'

'Yes, Sarah. I'll try to be fair, and I'll start with you. To whom did God give the Ten Commandments?'

'To His people, the Jews.'

'How did He give them to them, Paul?'

'God told them to Moses and Moses wrote them down.'

'Do you know where they're found in the Bible, Sarah?'

'We had to learn them from Exodus, chapter 20. But I think they're written down somewhere else too.'

'Yes, in the book of Deuteronomy. Why do you think God gave the commandments to His people?'

It was Paul's turn to answer. He thought for a moment and said, 'So the people would try to obey them and do what God wanted them to do.'

'More than that, I think, Paul. What is a commandment?'

'Something you must obey; something like an order.'

'Do you have to obey any other sort of commandment?'

'Yes, at school and at home too. Our teacher gives us some, and so do you.'

Missing her turn, Sarah interrupted, 'Like when you told us to do the dishwashing.'

Mr MacDonald laughed. 'Why then, Sarah, do you think you have rules and laws at school?'

'To stop us from getting into trouble?' Sarah answered enquiringly.

'More than that! What would school be like if everyone did as they liked?'

'Wonderful!' shouted Paul.

'Not really,' Sarah replied. 'It would be horrible. No one would enjoy it at all.'

Mr MacDonald nodded in agreement. 'God has given us His commandments to help us. They help us to understand what God is like. They tell us that He's good and kind and that He hates evil. They also tell us how we can please Him and show our love for Him. They show how we can live happily together.'

Paul often found it hard to be well-behaved. He didn't really think it would be fun to have no rules at school and he knew it was silly to play with plates when drying them, but somehow he acted stupidly at times. He wondered whether grown-ups found it as hard as he did to do the right thing.

'Are the Ten Commandments easy for you to obey, Dad?' Paul asked.

'No, they're not. Can you think of any commandment you've broken, Sarah?'

'The one about being jealous?'

'Which commandment is that?'

'I've forgotten. Is it the "covet" one? Yes. It is. Mum explained to me what "covet" means.'

'What happens if we don't keep God's law, Paul?'

'God isn't pleased with us,' said Paul.

The twins' father was pleased with the thoughtful answers they were giving to his questions. 'Has anyone ever kept all of God's commandments, children?'

'No,' they said.

'Are you sure that no one - absolutely no one - has?'

Paul guessed what his father meant. 'Jesus did.'

'What's the punishment we deserve if we break God's laws?'

'To die, to be punished, and never go to heaven?' Sarah asked.

'Yes,' agreed her father. 'Why did the Lord Jesus have to die, then, if He had kept God's laws.'

'To take our sins away.'

'All right, but what are our sins?'

'The things we do when we disobey the Ten Commandments,' Sarah answered.

'Very good, Sarah. If we try to obey the Ten Commandments, will we go to heaven?'

'No. We can go to heaven only if we trust in the Lord Jesus.'

Mrs MacDonald had been listening to the questions and answers and was impressed by all she heard. 'May I ask the twins a question now? Can we forget all about the Ten Commandments when we've trusted in the Lord Jesus as our Saviour?'

'Of course not,' said the twins in chorus.

11

Mr MacDonald wondered how he could show the twins the importance of the Ten Commandments in a way that would interest them. He knew that some of the words were difficult.

'Are there words you can't understand in the commandments?' he asked, thinking of something he would like the twins to do. 'What about adultery?'

'I'm not sure about that, Dad. Is it like coveting?'

'Yes, Sarah. It's like stealing too. It means taking someone else's husband or wife and treating him or her as your own.'

'Like David?' asked Sarah.

Mr MacDonald looked surprised. 'When did you hear that?'

'In church last Sunday in the sermon. David took Bathsheba and then he murdered her husband.'

The twins' mother laughed with pleasure. 'Mr Hill would be pleased to know that you listened to his sermon to the adults as well as the children's talk.'

'Well, you keep on listening like that, Sarah, and you too, Paul,' encouraged Mr MacDonald. 'Would you like me to talk to you about the Ten Commandments as I once did about the Lord's Prayer?'

'That's a good idea,' said Sarah.

'We could make it a project like last time,' suggested Paul.

'Good. The Ten Commandments are always important. Every day things happen which show how important they are. Tomorrow I'll give you each a note-book. On the first page write out the first commandment and then leave two pages. Then write out the second commandment and leave another two pages. Go on like this through the note-book until you've written down the tenth commandment.'

'What then, Dad?' asked Paul, getting interested.

'During the week, I want us to notice anything which shows us how important the Ten Commandments are.'

'What kind of things?'

'Well, Paul, if something happens at home which shows us how important they are, we'll take note of it. If we read something in the newspaper or hear something on the TV we'll write it down. And if we see something when we go out which helps us to understand them, we'll talk about that too.'

'Sounds good,' said Sarah.

'I'm looking forward to it,' Paul added.

'And our half-term holiday starts tomorrow too!' shouted Sarah.

2 Visit to a Museum

'I don't think I'll go to work today!' Mr MacDonald said the next morning, pretending that he'd just made up his mind not to go. 'It will be much better staying at home with you.'

'I know what's happening,' said Paul, 'you're taking some days off from work while we're home from school.'

Paul was right.   Mr MacDonald had a couple of days' holiday left and he had to use them up before the end of March.   He had arranged to take these last two days while the twins were on holiday.

Sarah was delighted. 'We can go to places together, Dad.'

'That's just what I plan to do,' laughed Mr MacDonald. 'If it's dry we'll go on a long walk, but if it's wet perhaps we'll go to a museum. I'm afraid it looks as if the rain is here to stay.'

'Then we'll have to save the long walk for another day, Dad,' suggested Paul.

* * *

Mrs MacDonald provided a quick breakfast because the twins were impatient to go. They even made their own beds when their mother said she couldn't go until their beds were made.

'I'll get the car out, Helen,' Mr MacDonald told his wife. And in a few minutes the whole family was ready for their outing. The MacDonald family had a new car - at least it was only two months old.

'Have you got your note-books, twins?' asked Mrs MacDonald. 'You might see something that you'll want to write down.'

'Yes. Dad gave them to us,' answered Sarah for them both.

'You'll need the wipers on, Dad,' said Paul. 'You know I've just been thinking,' he continued.

'What?'

'Well, you're not as fussy about this car now that we've had it a little while. When you first bought it, we all had to be very careful where we put our feet, and things like that!'

Mrs MacDonald laughed and Mr MacDonald smiled grudgingly.

'Poor old Dad,' Mrs MacDonald said. 'But you're quite right, Paul. We're often like that with new things. We have to be careful that we don't make a god out of the car and almost worship it.'

'What do you mean, Mum?'

16

'Well, Sarah, a thing like a car can become so important to you that you can make it seem as important as God.'

'Could you really?'

'Don't you remember the man who lived across the road where we used to live before?'

Paul and Sarah nodded. 'We watched him out of the window,' they said.

'What did he do?'

'Every morning before he went to work he cleaned the large secondhand car he had bought. Then when he came home each evening, he would come out and wipe the car again if it rained. Every Sunday he would spend half the day cleaning and polishing it.'

Mrs MacDonald nodded. 'You've got good memories,' she said. 'Now, I'm not saying that he did worship his car. That's not for us to say, but people used to say that all he thought about was his car.'

Paul remembered something else. 'I remember when some boys were playing football in the street. Their ball hit the radiator while Mr Forrester was cleaning it. He swore at them, and I remember you told us to stop looking out of the window and never to use God's name like that.'

The twins' father had been listening to the conversation as they drove along and he said, 'You've got at least two things to write down in your note-books.'

'Swearing goes down under the commandment not to take God's name in vain, doesn't it? That's the third commandment.'

'Yes, Sarah, some forms of swearing do. You could draw a picture of a man chasing boys away from his car, to remind you that it is when we're angry that we may be tempted to use wrong words.'

'Don't forget to write down that we shouldn't put things before God,' said Mrs MacDonald. 'That's the first commandment - "You shall have no other gods before Me." Our neighbour seemed to give as much time to his car as Dad and I give to praying to God and reading His Word.'

Mr MacDonald agreed. 'My car seemed very important when I first got it,' he confessed. 'I wanted to go out and show it off. But that was wrong.'

'Why, Dad?' asked Paul.

'Well, we should love God most, not cars and things. You could make the same mistake, couldn't you?'

'How?' asked Sarah.

Their father continued to explain. 'If you put a thing first in your life, it can easily become a kind of god to you. As we go along in the car, look in the windows of the different shops and stores and see if you can spot things that people may sometimes think more of than God.'

'Shall we put it on the page where we've written the first commandment, Dad?'

'Yes, that's a good idea.'

After they had driven for about ten more minutes, Mr MacDonald said, 'We'll soon be there now, twins. Let's hear your list, Sarah.'

Sarah began, 'Clothes, pets, and food.'

'Yes,' interrupted her mother. 'In the Bible the apostle Paul talks about people who make their stomach into a kind of god because all they think about is food and drink.'

'Jewellery,' continued Sarah, 'records and television. You can easily make a kind of god out of television, by watching all the time so you don't do other things.'

'A good list,' commended Mr MacDonald. 'Anything to add, Paul?'

'I had everything on Sarah's list except jewellery and I also wrote down bikes.'

Sarah had been thinking about the first

19

commandment and she said. 'But these aren't the only things the commandment means, are they? Moses didn't know anything about cars and TV.'

They all laughed. 'No,' answered her father, 'but in the country they had lived in - Egypt - the Israelites had seen many of the gods which the Egyptians worshipped. And in the country they were to be taken to - Canaan - they would find lots of heathen gods as well.'

Suddenly Mr MacDonald stopped talking. Then he said, 'No more for now, twins; we're here. We need a place to park. Keep your eyes open.'

Sarah saw a place first. Soon they were getting out of the car and heading for the museum.

First they went to the Egyptian rooms. The first room they went into seemed absolutely packed with Egyptian mummies.

'Why are they called mummies?' Sarah asked.

'To mummify is to stop a body from decaying by wrapping it with spices. So bodies which have been treated in this way are called mummies.'

'What even if they are really daddies, Dad?'

Paul joked.

Sarah peered into one of the boxes, or coffins, in which a mummy had been found. 'What are all those ornaments doing there? And look at those funny little figures! And see that beautiful silver and gold man. What's he?'

The twins' father came across the room and looked. 'Don't shout, Sarah. Everyone's looking at us! The man in charge will ask us to leave!'

He bent down and examined the objects in the glass case. 'Those ornaments are things the Egyptians believed the dead person would need in the new life he had gone to. Those funny little figures were supposed to work for the dead person in his new country. And I think that that silver and gold man was one of the Egyptian gods.'

Mrs MacDonald had joined them. 'That would be one of the gods the Lord meant when He said the Israelites weren't to have any other gods before Him.'

'Yes,' agreed her husband. 'The Israelites had just come out of Egypt when God gave them the commandment. And they had seen lots of false gods there - just like this one.'

'Were they real gods, Dad?'

'No, Sarah. They had no power, for there's only one true God. He's the God of the Bible and the Father of our Lord Jesus. Because He's the only true God, He tells us not to worship anything or anybody else as God.'

3   Skeletons and Nightmares

The rainy day seemed to have brought out lots of people to the museum.

'How many Egyptian rooms are there, Dad?'

'Four, I think, Sarah.'

'It would be easy to get lost here,' commented Paul.

His mother nodded her head in agreement. 'This is the main building, upper floor, north. There must be dozens of different rooms. This is the second Egyptian room.'

Paul and Sarah walked ahead to look at some of the display cases to the right-hand side of the large room.   A group of boys and girls from a school had just arrived.   One teacher was in charge of them, on her own, and she was having a hard job keeping them quiet. Some of the boys ran from showcase to showcase, and the attendant in his dark blue uniform was eyeing them suspiciously.

'Now look here, boys,' he said, 'stop running about, or else I'll have to send you out.'

The boys looked a little subdued and came to look at the same showcase as Paul and Sarah. Inside there was a human skeleton placed exactly as it had been found in a kind of large coffin. The person's legs were all bent up, and a notice explained that this was the way in which people were often buried in ancient times.

'Oooh!' moaned one of the boys, pretending to be afraid. Then in a shrill voice he cried, 'This will give me nightmares!' At every case he came to, Paul and Sarah heard him say the same thing, until the teacher came and whispered something in his ear which made him stop.

'I wonder what she said to him, Paul?'

'Something that shut him up, anyway.'

'It's sort of scary here, isn't it? I wouldn't like to be here at night on my own with all those mummies!'

Paul tried to look brave and superior. 'Well, you're only a girl! But, of course, I wouldn't mind.'

The twins' parents had come up behind them and they smiled. 'Oh, really, Paul. I'm not so sure about that!' retorted his father. 'But come and look over here. There's something else for you to write in your books about the Ten Commandments.'

In a large glass case which extended the whole length of a wall, there were dozens of objects made of silver and gold. Many of them were animals and birds. A notice explained that all these objects were gods which the Egyptians had worshipped. In the centre there was a golden calf. Mr MacDonald pointed to it.

'What does that remind you of? And which commandment does it illustrate?'

Sarah guessed first. 'The golden calf which the Israelites worshipped when Moses was up the mountain.'

'And which commandment?'

'The second. I think I can remember it. Wait a moment. Yes, I know: "You shall not make for yourself an idol in the form of anything". Is that right?'

Mr MacDonald smiled. 'Yes, fine,' he congratulated Sarah. 'You tell us the story then, Paul.'

'I'll try,' answered Paul, secretly wishing he had been first to mention the golden calf so that it would have been Sarah's turn to do something. But he had a good memory for Bible stories and he enjoyed telling them.

'Moses was talking to God on the mountain of Sinai,' began Paul. 'All the people were waiting for Moses to come down. They got fed up with waiting because he was such a long time. So some of them said to Aaron, "Come on, make us some god to go in front of us. We don't know what's happened to Moses." Well, Aaron listened to them and told them to bring him all the golden earrings the people wore. Then he made a metal calf from them. Then I think Aaron built an altar in front of the golden calf and all the people worshipped it. I can't remember what happened then, except that God was very angry.'

'You've done very well,' said Mrs MacDonald.

His father agreed. 'One of the things the Israelites found most difficult to avoid was idolatry. Idolatry is the worship of idols. They had seen so many in Egypt that they thought their God - the only true God - could be worshipped in the same way.'

Mrs MacDonald knew this commandment wasn't easy to understand, so she said, 'You ought to explain, David, why God was so strict about this.'

Her husband nodded. 'God is a Spirit. He is invisible. He can't be enclosed in a space, as you and I can be. Nothing that man can make with his hands can show what God is like.'

Sarah and Paul were trying hard to understand. Paul understood how stupid it was to make an image of God the Father, because no one has ever seen Him. But he knew that Jesus is God, too.

'What about Jesus, then, Dad?' he asked. 'People saw Him when He was on earth. Is it wrong to make a picture or statue of Him?'

'If we use it to worship God with, Paul, it's wrong. Anyway, no one knows what the Lord Jesus looked like. And, even if someone did, it's not what the Lord Jesus looked like that matters, but the kind of person He is. What God says is quite clear: He wants us to worship Him without using statues, carvings and pictures to help. One of the reasons is that probably these things could become so important to us that we might think them more important than God Himself. So we're better without them.'

Mr MacDonald looked at his watch. 'Only twenty minutes more, twins. My parking meter will be running out of time. Just a little longer, and then home!'

As they left the museum, the MacDonald family visited the bookstall in the front hall of the museum. They bought a postcard each.

28

Sarah was thrilled to be able to buy a photograph of the silver and gold figure of one of the idols which Paul and she had sketched in their notebooks.

With about four minutes to spare before their parking time ran out, they arrived at the car. Soon they were on their way home.

4 Detective Work

As it wasn't a very pleasant morning and they didn't have to go to school, their mother had let the twins sleep a little longer. Their father had just finished his breakfast and was about to put on his raincoat when they came downstairs.

'Have a good day, twins,' Mr MacDonald said.

'I don't know what we're going to do, Dad,' complained Sarah. 'It's so wet. We won't be able to play outside or do anything at all.'

'Well, you could always help your mother,' suggested Mr MacDonald. 'You could even do some of her shopping for her. Look, I know what you can do this morning if it keeps on raining. Get your Ten Commandments book and look at the next commandment. Write underneath what you think it means and do a couple of drawings that will remind you of the meaning. If you would like to colour them, I'll say whose is the better when I come home this evening.'

After breakfast, Paul and Sarah helped clear the table so that they could spread out their books and pencils.

'We're going to start thinking about the next commandment, Mum,' explained Sarah, who was sitting at one end of the table.

'What is the commandment this time?'

' "You shall not misuse the name of the Lord your God",' Sarah replied.

'What do you think that means?' asked Mrs MacDonald.

'I don't know, really,' answered Sarah, looking puzzled. 'I think it has something to do with swearing.'

'What's swearing?'

'Well, isn't it something that God doesn't want you to say?' suggested Paul, from the other end of the table.

'In a way,' agreed his mother. 'But God doesn't want us to say angry words, and angry words are not the same as swearing, are they?'

'No, I suppose they're not,' agreed Sarah. 'You tell us then, please.'

'Some kinds of swearing are an insult to God, because His name is used wrongly.'

'What's an insult?' asked Paul.

'Suppose someone said to you, "Paul, you come from a dreadful home!" How would you feel about that?'

'I'd be angry.'

'Yes,' agreed Sarah. 'And it wouldn't be true, would it?'

'I hope not,' laughed Mrs MacDonald. 'To insult someone is to say something about him that isn't true, and something that hurts that person's reputation. Taking God's name in vain means saying something about God that isn't true, or hurting His reputation so that people don't think about Him in the right way. The commandment means several things really. It has to do with an oath. Do you know what an oath is?'

'Something like a promise?' suggested Sarah.

'Yes. It's a promise, or some words which you say you want God to listen to, like when a person is in court.'

'I know,' said Paul. 'We've played that at school.'

'Yes,' agreed Sarah, 'and we've seen it on television too.'

'Can you remember what a person has to say in court when he or she is going to give evidence?' Mrs MacDonald asked.

'I think so,' Paul said slowly. 'Doesn't it go something like this: "I swear by Almighty God that the evidence I shall give shall be the truth,

34

the whole truth, and nothing but the truth"?'
He looked pleased with himself at getting it
right.

Mrs MacDonald continued, 'If someone
swears, or promises to tell the truth as if he were
telling it only to God, and then tells a lie, he's
misused God's name - he hasn't really meant
what he said about God.'

Mrs MacDonald thought for a moment.
'The Lord Jesus had something to say about
swearing. If you'll get me my Bible, please,
Sarah, you can read it to us. It was part of the
Sermon on the Mount.'

Sarah brought her Bible and Mrs
MacDonald found the place for her. Sarah
read aloud carefully, 'Do not swear at all: either
by heaven, for it is God's throne; or by the earth,
for it is His footstool; or by Jerusalem, for it is
the city of the Great King. And do not swear
by your head, for you cannot make even one
hair white or black. Simply let your "Yes" be
"Yes", and your "No", "No"; anything beyond
this comes from the evil one.'

'I still don't understand,' said Paul.

'We sometimes say things without
thinking,' explained the twins' mother. 'And
often we bring God's name into things without

meaning to and without thinking what we say. God wants us not to sin in what we do - or say.'

Sarah remembered her book. 'What do you think we ought to put in our book? Dad said to write something underneath the commandment to explain.'

'Put "We should honour God's name". I'm sure if you went out this morning and listened to people talking you would find words being said which break this commandment. Why don't you do that? You could do some shopping for me.'

This idea - a kind of detective work - suddenly made the shopping sound interesting.

'I want some cheese and eggs,' continued Mrs MacDonald. 'You could go to the supermarket for me. Just listen to anything you hear people say, and see if I'm right. I would be glad, though, if you proved me wrong.'

When they arrived at the supermarket, it was full of people. 'I think some of them have come in to get out of the rain,' whispered Paul.

A mother was walking in front of the twins, with her little girl. The shopping trollies which a child could sit in were all being used and she had to hold the little girl's hand.

The little girl touched everything whenever

her mother let go of her hand. At the end of one counter stood a huge pile of cans arranged in a kind of pyramid.

'I hope she doesn't touch those, Paul.'

But she did! The little girl tried to get a can of baked beans from the middle. She pulled it out and - crash! Down tumbled lots of cans of baked beans! The mother shouted and used God's name. Then she spanked the little girl, who began to cry.

Paul and Sarah didn't need to look at one another; they had both heard the mother misuse God's name. The little girl couldn't understand what her mother meant, and the mother probably didn't realise she had been using God's name.

On their way home, Paul and Sarah discussed what they could draw in their books. They had learned more about the third commandment than they thought they would in one small shopping expedition. Paul drew a man in a witness-box and the words coming out of his mouth - as in a comic - "I swear by Almighty God that the evidence I shall give shall be the truth, the whole truth, and nothing but the truth," and Sarah drew a picture of an angry mother spanking her little girl, and all the cans of baked beans on the floor.

5 A Paper Delivery

During very windy weather, part of the concrete wall which went around the front garden of the MacDonalds' house had been blown down. The twins' father wanted to repair it so that none of it would fall down on anyone passing by.

'May I mix the cement?' asked Paul.

'Yes, all right, provided you are careful! Put your boots on.'

'I'd like to help too,' said Sarah.

'You can't mix the cement - that's a boy's job,' crowed Paul.

'No, it isn't,' answered Sarah.

'Stop arguing, you two,' interrupted Mr MacDonald. 'Perhaps you could fill the watering can for me, please, Sarah, and I would be grateful if you would get the broom and sweep up as we go along. First of all, we must get the cement and the tools we need out of the garage.'

Sarah remembered something. 'Dad, I saw Mr Ross mending his wall last Sunday morning. The wind must have blown down some of his wall too. You wouldn't repair your wall on a Sunday, would you, Dad?'

'No, I wouldn't,' agreed her father. 'That's where the Ten Commandments come in again to help us. The fourth commandment is, "Remember the Sabbath day by keeping it holy". It then goes on to tell us that we're not to work ourselves or to make other people work on Sunday, if we can avoid it. I know I should keep Sunday very special and free from all the odd jobs that could so easily fill it.'

'Why, Dad?' asked Paul.

'Well, "sabbath" means "to rest". When God made the world, how many days did it take?'

'Six.'

'What did He do on the seventh day?'

'He rested,' answered Paul again. 'But, Dad, Sunday is the first day of the week, not the last.'

'You're quite right,' agreed Mr MacDonald. 'Saturday was the day the Jews kept to remember God's creation. But Christians have kept Sunday, the first day of the week, because it was on the first day of the week that the Lord Jesus rose again from the dead. So on Sundays we remember that God made the world and, second, that the Lord Jesus rose again and lives today.'

40

'I remember Mr Hill telling us in church that that's why he often starts the service with a hymn about Jesus rising from the dead,' commented Sarah.

'Yes, I remember that too,' said Mr MacDonald. 'God wants Sunday to be a special day and the one we like most. Now it can't be a special day if we go to work as we do on all the other days. And so God doesn't want us to work on Sunday unless the work is something that needs to be done to help someone in difficulty.'

'What about doing things like cleaning my teeth, Dad?'

'Oh, yes, Paul, you should clean your teeth on Sundays.'

'What about cleaning my shoes?' asked Sarah.

'Well, that's something you could do on Saturday, so it would be better to clean them then.'

'What's the difference between teeth and shoes, Dad?'

'That's easy, Sarah. You need to clean your teeth every day and you can't clean them twice in one day to make do for the next! But you can clean your shoes the night before so that they're clean for the next day.'

Paul had been thinking about Mr Ross and the other people he had seen working on Sundays. 'But if some people didn't do all their odd jobs on Sundays, what would they do with themselves all day?'

'You tell me, Paul. What do you think they ought to do on Sundays?'

'I suppose they ought to go to church to worship God.'

'Yes,' said Sarah, 'on Sundays we have more time to read the Bible and to pray to God together.'

'What do you like most of all on a Sunday?' enquired the twins' father.

'I like going to Sunday school and meeting all my friends there,' answered Sarah.

'And it's good because you don't have to go to work,' added Paul.

Mr MacDonald nodded. 'What do you think life would be like if we worked all the time?'

Sarah thought for a moment. 'I suppose if we just worked and worked, we would get more and more tired - and very ill.'

Mr MacDonald agreed. 'All of God's laws have a purpose. God made our bodies and He knows they need a rest each week from normal work.'

While the twins had been talking with their father, they had been collecting the things they needed. 'I'll have to drive the car out to get at the cement,' Mr MacDonald thought aloud. 'Would you like to open the garage doors, please, Paul?'

'I'll sit in the car with you,' said Sarah.

When they were in the car, Mr MacDonald remembered something. 'Oh, Sarah, get out my record book, please. It's in the glove compartment.'

'What's that, Dad?'

'That book with things like tickets in it.'

'What's it for?'

'The makers of the car gave it to me when I bought the car. It tells me how often my car has to go to the garage for servicing and what they will need to do to it.'

'How often does it have to go to the garage to have a service?'

'Every six thousand miles.'

'What would happen if you didn't take it in?'

Her father thought for a moment. 'After a while the engine wouldn't work properly. If you don't stop using a car every now and again to let the garage grease it and take care of it, it will not only break down but it will become dangerous to drive.'

'Our bodies are a bit like machines,' commented Sarah. 'God gives us one day to rest after six days of work.'

'Very good,' agreed her father. 'And people's health does break down and they become ill if they don't keep God's law. Of course, there are some people who have to work on Sundays. I expect you can think of some.'

'Doctors, nurses, firemen and policemen,' suggested Sarah.

'Yes, and lots of others,' said Mr MacDonald. 'But when they work on Sunday, they have a day off some other time.'

By the time they had driven the car out and shut the garage doors, Paul was already mixing the cement. He was getting himself pretty messy with it.

'Just as well you had your boots on,' commented his father.

Very quickly, Mr MacDonald worked with the cement, and every now and again he would stop, as one of the neighbours passing by stopped to talk with him. Paul and Sarah were particularly glad when they saw Roger come round the corner on his bicycle. Roger was in the twins' father's Bible class, and he often came over. The twins liked him. He was a few years older than they were and he went to the school Paul hoped to go to some day.

'Hello, Roger,' exclaimed Mr MacDonald. 'You don't look very happy. What's wrong?'

'Oh, I've a problem, Mr MacDonald,' complained Roger. 'I'd like to talk it over with you.'

'Fine, would you like us to go inside somewhere on our own?'

'Oh, no,' replied Roger. 'The twins can hear about it. You see, I wanted to do a newspaper delivery round.'

'That's a good idea.'

'I thought so too,' said Roger. 'And my dad said it would give me some pocket money. I've just had my thirteenth birthday and that means I'm old enough. Mr Johnson, the newsagent, says that I can start next week if I like. You're only allowed to work six days a week. But before I start I've got to get a form signed by my parents and my teacher at school.'

'Nothing difficult about that, Roger,' commented Mr MacDonald. 'Why are you

looking so miserable?'

'Well, it means working on a Sunday, and I don't know what to say. I know I shouldn't, but I do want to earn some money.'

'I thought you said you only had to work six days.'

'Yes, but Sunday is the busiest day and that's when Mr Johnson likes the boys to work most of all. I've heard them say so.'

Paul had been listening carefully. 'Why is it the busiest day?'

His father explained, 'People have more time to read on a Sunday, and lots of larger newspapers and magazines come out at weekends. What do you think Roger ought to do, twins?'

'He shouldn't work on a Sunday if he can avoid it, should he, Dad?' said Sarah.

'What do you think yourself, Roger?' asked Mr MacDonald.

'No, I don't think I ought to, Mr MacDonald.'

'What! even if it means you can't have the job?' exclaimed Paul.

'I suppose so,' answered Roger. 'I do want to please the Lord.'

Mr MacDonald had an idea. 'You know,

Roger, I think Mr Johnson would be very understanding if you explained to him how you feel. I think you ought to tell him that you would like to work for him. But tell him too, that you don't feel happy about working on Sundays - not because there are so many papers to deliver, but because it's God's day. See if he will let you be one of the boys who work on the six other days. Why don't you go and see him now?'

'I'll come with you, Roger,' offered Paul.

'Thanks,' said Roger, and off they went.

Mr Johnson was much more sympathetic than Roger had ever guessed he would be. 'Why don't you want to work on a Sunday?'

'Well, Mr Johnson, I know it's God's day and as far as we can we shouldn't do our ordinary work then, and it's the day we should keep for worshipping and serving God. I would feel bad if I delivered papers on a Sunday.'

Mr Johnson nodded his head approvingly. 'I respect your honesty, Roger. I'll be glad to have you. You need not deliver papers for me on a Sunday. You can start next Monday. How's that?'

'Thank you!' exclaimed Roger. 'That's better than what I expected!'

6 Mums and Dads

'What are you doing now, Paul?' enquired his mother, as she came into the dining room and saw the twins drawing in their Ten Commandments books.

'We're both drawing a picture of Roger delivering newspapers,' he explained, 'and underneath Dad suggested that we write, "Six days of work, and one of rest".'

'That's a good idea,' agreed Mrs MacDonald. 'Dad was telling me all about your talk with Roger.'

At this moment Mr MacDonald joined them, all ready to take the family out for a drive. He winked at his wife as she looked at him. 'I'm looking forward to the next commandment, Helen, aren't you?' he asked in a deep voice.

Mrs MacDonald thought for a second or two, and then she realised what he meant.

'Yes, I am too.'

'Why, Dad?' asked Sarah.

'Well, it's all about you and Paul and Mum and me.'

'Oh, I know,' said Paul. 'It's "Honour your father and your mother"!'

'Do you think you know what it means,

Paul?'

'I think so, Dad. Doesn't it mean that we should thank our parents?'

'What for?'

'All the things you do for us.'

'You tell me some of the things I do!' suggested Mr MacDonald.

'You help us. You do things with us. You take us places.'

'That's kind of you, Paul,' laughed his father. 'What are you doing, Sarah? Oh, I see,' he added, as he saw that Sarah was turning the pages of her dictionary to discover what the word "honour" meant.

'It says, "To respect, to look up to, to admire".'

Mr MacDonald nodded his head in agreement. 'What's the most important thing for children to do for their parents then?'

'To be obedient to them?' Sarah answered, as if asking a question.

'Yes, I'm sure that's right. The apostle Paul wrote to the children at Ephesus and said the right thing for them to do was to obey their parents as those whom God had given them to teach them and to bring them up. And then he went on to quote the fifth commandment.'

Mrs MacDonald thought that she would try to help. 'May I ask a difficult question - perhaps an embarrassing one?' she asked, smiling.

The children nodded.

'Do you like obeying your parents?'

'Oh, yes,' replied Paul.

'Always?'

'Well, not always.'

'When don't you like obeying?'

'Sometimes you make us go upstairs for things, like our shoes.'

'Whose fault is it that you don't wear your shoes?' the twins' mother asked.

'Oh, it's ours,' answered Sarah.

'When else don't you like obeying?'

'I don't like going to bed when I'm told, sometimes,' grumbled Paul.

'Are you ever disobedient?'

'You know we are, Mum!' Sarah said.

'Is that right or wrong?' questioned Mrs MacDonald.

'Oh, it's wrong because God says we should honour and obey our parents,' replied Sarah.

'Can you think of anything children shouldn't do to their parents, Paul?'

Paul thought for a moment. 'They

shouldn't be rude.'

'I know,' interrupted Sarah. 'We shouldn't shout or talk when you're talking to someone else. Paul sometimes interrupts.'

'Oh, Sarah,' cried Mrs MacDonald, 'that's really not fair, is it, Dad? She's just as bad as Paul!'

Paul looked pleased that his parents were sticking up for him.

'I'm sorry,' said Sarah.

Mr MacDonald looked at the clock. 'It's time we got going. We'll go and see Grandma first. We want to find out if she'll come and visit us.'

'Why do you go to Grandma's so often, Dad?' Sarah asked.

'Since Grand-dad died, Grandma has been lonely, and when our parents grow old and have any kind of need, it's up to us to help to look after them. They may need money or a home. And they always need our love. Although I'm much older than you, I need to honour my mother just as much as you need to honour Mum and me.'

*   *   *

When the twins arrived at their grandmother's, they could tell at once that she

52

was pleased to see them all.

'Do you want us to do any shopping, Mum?' asked Mr MacDonald.

'No, thank you. One of the neighbours got me all I needed. Where are you all going?'

'We're going to the park, Grandma.'

'Would you like to come with us?' Mrs MacDonald asked.

'Oh, I don't think so, dear. It's rather cold for me. But I'm so glad that you came to see me. I'll look forward to coming on Friday. Wait a moment, twins, before you go. I've something for you in the cupboard.'

The twins guessed at once what it was. Grandma always seemed to have some chocolate or sweets ready for them whenever they came. They knew she would have some more ready for their next visit too!

It was really quite cold when they arrived at the park and there was a strong wind blowing.

'Look, Dad!' cried Paul. 'There's a man trying to fly a kite. What a good strong wind for it! May we go over and watch?'

On one side of the park there was a slight hill. The man, who was obviously the father of the small boy standing at the bottom, ran down the hill with the kite flying in the air behind him,

trying to get it airborne. But it was no use. The kite fell to the ground.

'Oh, dear!' exclaimed Paul. 'The centre piece has snapped in half.'

They watched and saw the small boy run to where the kite had fallen.

'Daddy, you've broken it!' shouted the boy. 'You're a stupid, terrible Daddy!'

'Now, that's not the way to talk to me,' answered his father.

'I don't care,' said the little boy. 'You don't know how to fly a kite. I'll tell Mummy.'

Mr MacDonald looked at Paul and Sarah and said quietly, 'Do you think that's the way to keep the fifth commandment?'

They shook their heads. 'No, we should never be rude or say things like that about our parents,' Sarah said.

'It's an important lesson to learn,' their father went on. 'I wish I had respected my parents more when I was younger.'

'Why, Dad?'

'Looking back, Paul, I know I could have done much more for them. They cared for me and put themselves out for me. I wish I had appreciated them more.'

7   A Great Surprise

The twins were especially excited.   They were going with their parents to visit the school their father had attended when he was young. Time just wouldn't go quickly enough that afternoon.   Eventually it was time for the twins and their mother to catch the train to town. They soon spotted their father when they got off the train at the place he'd said he would wait for them.

'Hello, Dad, we're ready!' exclaimed Paul.

'Good,' replied Mr MacDonald, 'so am I. Can we go and get a newspaper before we walk to the school?   You can get it for me if you like, Paul.'

Paul ran to where a man was selling newspapers.   By the side of the box he sat on was a placard with the news headlines. As Paul joined the people waiting in line he read, 'Another Man Charged in Murder Case'.

'Here you are, Dad,' said Paul, giving the paper to his father.   'There's been a murder or something.'

'I'm afraid there are too many of those,' sighed Mrs MacDonald.

Mr MacDonald glanced at the headlines as

he walked along. 'This looks like a particularly brutal one. Someone has been stabbed to death.'

'Murderers must be horrible people,' Sarah thought aloud.

'Well, I don't know,' corrected her father. 'One must be careful in saying that, Sarah. Sometimes murderers are very ordinary people like ourselves. We ought to be sorry for them. But murder is a dreadful thing, and that's why the sixth commandment says, "You shall not murder". Why do you think people commit murder, Paul?'

'Because they don't like people, I suppose.'

'Do you ever find yourself not liking people, Sarah?'

'Yes. There are some boys in my class I don't like sometimes.'

'Why?'

'They're mean.'

'What do they do?'

'They fight.'

'Do they hurt you? You're a girl.'

'Sometimes. They pull my hair and try to knock me over in the playground.'

'What do you do then?' asked her father.

'I don't do anything. I try to keep out of

their way.'

'What do you think we ought to do when we don't like someone, Paul?'

'I don't know, Dad.'

'The best thing we can do is to ask God to help us to like them,' suggested Mr MacDonald. 'I know it's not easy. But God will help us, if we really want Him to do so.'

The twins' excitement grew as they came near the school.

'Here it is!' explained Mr MacDonald, pointing to a rather old building. There was a blue board at the front, with the name of the school in gold lettering. 'Now, follow me,' he said.

When they stood inside the doors, there were lots of people going into the school auditorium. One of the senior boys politely asked the twins' father for the tickets, and then he led them to their seats. At one end of the auditorium there was a large stage. In the centre, near the stage, was another platform, and all the seats were grouped around this platform.

'May I have a look at the programme, please, Dad?' asked Paul.

'Yes,' said Mr MacDonald, 'and then you

will see what the play or, in fact, plays, are all about.'

Paul looked at the programme and found that they were going to see six miracle plays. 'What are miracle plays, Dad?'

His father explained. 'In the Middle Ages, and usually in the fifteenth and sixteenth centuries, too, in the towns and cities of England, the various groups of craftsmen would each put on a different play each year. Then, on a religious holiday, all the people in the town or city would spend the whole day in the streets as a procession of wagons would move about the town. On these wagons the plays would be performed again and again to different audiences in different places.'

'What were they all about, Dad?'

'The idea, Paul, was to tell the whole Bible story from creation to the last judgment. Now we must be quiet; it's going to start.'

The lights in the auditorium dimmed and went out, and the first half of the programme took place. It was all very well done.

The first play was the story of Cain and Abel, the second Noah's Ark, and the third Abraham and Isaac. Cain seemed a horrible fellow; he was cruel to the people who worked for him and he bullied his kind brother Abel. He was very jealous of Abel and in a fit of temper killed him.

Noah's Ark fascinated Sarah and Paul. The centre platform was used to build a huge ark before their very eyes. Then they felt like crying, when, later, Abraham prepared to kill Isaac, his son. They were so glad when the angel of the Lord stopped Abraham just in time.

Everyone clapped excitedly when the intermission came.

'Let's stretch our legs a bit,' suggested Mr MacDonald as the lights came on. 'There are refreshments downstairs. I'll show you where I used to eat school dinners!'

In the hall outside the auditorium Sarah and Paul saw a book in a glass stand. 'What's that, Dad?'

'That, Paul, is a list of former students who lost their lives in the two world wars. It's called a book of remembrance. One of the school teachers turns over a page every day.'

'Do you think it's wrong for men to be soldiers and fight?' asked Paul.

'Why do you ask?'

'I was thinking about the commandment, "You shall not murder".'

'Well, no, it's not wrong in the same way that murder is wrong. Soldiers are very necessary at times. Fighting a war for one's country isn't the same as committing murder. Murder is something private that one person deliberately does to another. A soldier who fights for his country because he's ordered to is not breaking the commandment, although, if he just killed because he enjoyed killing people then he would be breaking it. I ought to tell you, however, that some people think differently and they believe that to kill in war is the same as murder.'

The second half of the plays was as good as the first. This time the twins saw the Shepherds at Bethlehem, the Kings with their three gifts, and King Herod's Court. It was quite dark when they left the school, and Sarah and Paul felt very grown-up at being out so late.

'Did you enjoy it, twins?'

'Oh, yes, Dad!' they said, almost in chorus.

'The plays were very good,' agreed their mother.

'I didn't like either Cain or Herod, though!' Sarah said.

'They were both murderers, weren't they, Dad?'

Mr MacDonald nodded his head in agreement with Paul. 'Can you think of anyone else in the Bible who committed murder?'

'Moses,' suggested Sarah.

'And David did, really,' added Paul.

'Why did Cain kill his brother?' asked Mr MacDonald.

Sarah answered, 'Because he was jealous of him.'

'Your turn, Paul. Why did Moses kill the Egyptian?'

'He was angry because the Egyptian was cruel to one of Moses' people.'

'What about David, Sarah?'

'Well, he wanted something - or rather somebody's wife - who belonged to someone else.'

'Now not all of these men were evil men, were they?' asked Mr MacDonald.

'No, Moses and David weren't,' Paul said.

'Remember that,' stressed his father. 'Moses got angry, and David wanted something that didn't belong to him. Before they knew what they were doing, they committed murder. So never think that something like murder could never happen to you or me. The best way to keep this commandment is to love other people, no matter how hard it is. Only God can help us to do this. He wants us to respect life because He's given it to us.'

By the time Sarah and Paul were walking the last few hundred yards home, they were almost asleep on their feet.

'Dad, can God forgive a murderer?'

'Oh, yes,' Mr MacDonald assured Sarah. 'The Lord Jesus died on the cross for sinners, no matter what our sins may have been.'

Sarah was glad and with that thought she quickly went to sleep.

8   Finders not Keepers

When Grandma arrived on Friday morning the twins had a lot to tell her.

'You look very busy,' she said, as she saw them with their books spread out on the table and their pencil boxes open. 'May I have a look?'

'Of course,' replied Sarah.

Grandma looked over Sarah's shoulder. 'It looks like a king, Sarah.'

'That's right. It's King Herod ordering his soldiers to kill all the male children under two years of age in Bethlehem.'

'Oh, I can guess what your picture is, Paul,' Grandma said. 'It's Cain killing Abel, isn't it?'

'Yes,' confirmed Paul.

'It's a terrible sight!' exclaimed Grandma. 'What are you drawing these pictures for?'

'Dad had an idea,' explained Sarah. 'He's teaching us about the Ten Commandments. These are our Ten Commandments note-books. Dad usually explains the commandments and, where we can, we write down something about each one and we also draw a picture to help us to remember what we've learned.'

'A very good idea,' commented Grandma. 'But not all of the commandments are easy to understand are they?'

'No, but you could help us to do the next one, Grandma,' suggested Sarah.

'Oh, no, I'm not smart enough!'

'You are, Grandma!' assured Paul.

'What's the next one, then?'

' "You shall not commit adultery",' answered Paul.

'You've saved a difficult one for me, haven't you?'

'We know what adultery is, Grandma,' explained Sarah. 'We heard a sermon in church about David taking Bathsheba. Adultery means taking someone else's husband or wife and treating him or her as your own, doesn't it?'

'That's about right,' agreed Grandma. 'You tell me the story then, Paul.'

'I don't know if I can remember it all.'

'Just do your best.'

Paul began, 'One afternoon, David took a walk on the roof of his royal palace. From the roof he saw a woman bathing. She was very beautiful. So David sent one of his servants to find out who she was. Someone said, "That must be Bathsheba, the wife of Uriah." So David sent messengers to bring her to him. She came and he slept with her as if she were his wife. Then she went home.'

'What happened then?' asked Grandma, seeing that Paul was faltering.

'I know,' said Sarah. 'A little while later, Bathsheba sent a message and told David that she was expecting a baby because he had treated her as if she had been his wife. The next part of the story is rather difficult to remember.'

'Try,' suggested Grandma.

'Well, David wanted Uriah to think that he, Uriah, was the father of Bathsheba's baby, so that he wouldn't know anything about what David had done. But things didn't work out like that. So David decided he would have to get rid of Uriah.'

'That was when David committed murder,' interrupted Paul. 'He wrote a letter to the general in charge of the army and told him to put Uriah in the front line where the fighting would be most dangerous. He was to be suddenly left on his own so that the enemy would kill him. And Uriah was killed.'

Sarah had been thinking. 'It's not a very pleasant story, is it, Grandma?'

'No', agreed Grandma. 'But because these things really happened, the Bible tells us about them. David didn't stop looking at Bathsheba when he was tempted; he ought to have looked away. His eyes gave him wrong thoughts to turn into actions. He brought a lot of unhappiness to himself and to others.'

'I feel sorry for Uriah,' said Paul.

Just then Mrs MacDonald walked over to the table to see what the twins were doing. 'It looks like you're learning more for your book,' she said, looking pleased.

'Yes,' added Grandma, 'the twins and I are having a good time.'

'I've an idea,' Mrs MacDonald suggested. 'Why don't you go home with Grandma this afternoon when she leaves. You could spend some more time with her and then Dad could pick you up there on his way home from work.'

The wide grins on the twins' faces showed that they thought it was a good idea too. And Mrs MacDonald knew that Grandma would enjoy having their company. Before they left that afternoon Mrs MacDonald asked the twins to do her a favour.

'I know what you could do for me, twins,' she suggested. 'On your way home with Dad, you could stop at the supermarket and get some things I want for tomorrow. Please write a list for me, Sarah. Can you find a scrap of paper?'

Sarah thought for a moment where she could find some paper. Then she remembered that her school exercise book was on the dining room table. Grandma was writing a letter.

'What are you doing, Sarah?' she asked in surprise, as she saw Sarah was about to tear the centre pages from her exercise book.

'Mum wants me to write down her shopping list,' explained Sarah.

'But whose book is that?'

'It's my school book.'

'Then it doesn't belong to you, does it?'

'Well, it's mine, in a way.'

'But does it really belong to you or the school?'

'The school.'

'Then that's really a kind of stealing, Sarah,' explained Grandma. 'I'm sure your mother wouldn't want you to do that. You may have a sheet of my notepaper instead.'

'I hadn't thought that stealing included taking paper out of a school exercise book, Grandma,' Sarah said. 'I wouldn't have done it if I'd known.'

'Remember then,' explained Grandma. 'This kind of thing is as wrong as stealing big things.'

'What! Like someone stealing a car or some jewels?'

'Just the same, Sarah. God wants us to respect one another's property. That's why the eighth commandment says, "You shall not steal". So if you borrow a book, make sure you return it. If you don't, it's just like stealing it. If you go into a supermarket and you're given too much change, don't go away glad that you received too much, but take it back. If you don't you're really stealing.'

'I suppose climbing over people's fences and taking apples off their trees is stealing,' suggested Sarah.

Grandma nodded her head.

Later Sarah and Paul walked with Grandma to the bus stop. When the bus came, it was quite full. Grandma and Sarah found seats and Paul stood by them. They had to go only a short way. When they got off the bus, Grandma explained that she wanted to go into the police station across the road.

'Into the police station!' cried Paul with surprise.

'Don't look so horrified,' she pleaded with a smile. 'The other week I found a purse and I took it into the police station. It had some money in it. They told me to return in a week or two to see if the purse had been claimed.'

Paul and Sarah were glad to see the inside of a police station. They hoped they might see the cells, but they were disappointed. They went into a large room with a long counter, behind which stood a police sergeant.

'Good afternoon,' he said, 'what can I do for you?'

Grandma MacDonald explained why she had come. The sergeant looked up the record in a book. 'Yes,' he said, 'it has been claimed. Thank you for bringing it in so promptly. The owner came in the other day.'

As they left the police station, Sarah asked, 'What would have happened if the owner hadn't claimed the purse, Grandma?'

'The purse and the money would have been given to me.'

'You could have kept them in the beginning, Grandma,' Paul said. 'You didn't have to take them to the police station. We say, "Finders keepers" at school.'

'That's not a good saying, Paul. Not to take

it to the police would have been a kind of stealing.   And I'm glad that the owner has claimed the purse. Wouldn't you be glad if you discovered that something you had lost had been handed in at the police station?'

The twins nodded their head in agreement.

9   True or False?

Sunday was the MacDonald family's favourite day.   One of the things which the twins looked forward to in the fine weather was the walk they had in the afternoon. As they set off for their usual walk, they suddenly heard a tremendous screech of car brakes.

'Look at that, Dad!' shouted Paul.   A motorcycle had come down the road at a tremendous speed, much faster than the speed limit. To make room for the motorcycle as it passed at a bend, a car swerved into the pavement and, in doing so, hit a parked car. A horrible sound of grinding metal followed. The motor-cyclist didn't stop but continued straight on.

'It's too far to see the number plate of that motor-cycle, Dad,' said Paul.

The twins' father ran over to where the two cars were. No one was hurt. The owner of the parked car came out of the house and he was furious. He started to shout at the driver of the other car.

'It wasn't his fault,' explained Mr MacDonald.   'We saw it.   It was the motor-cyclist's fault.   He was travelling at a terrific speed.'

'Did you see it all?' asked the driver of the car which had had to swerve.

'Most of it,' said Mr MacDonald.

'Would you be a witness then, please?'

'Of course,' answered Mr MacDonald.

'May I have your name and address?'

So Mr MacDonald gave both the owners his name and address, and the owners exchanged the names of their insurance companies.

As they walked back to the park a few minutes later, Paul asked, 'Why did that driver want you to be a witness?'

'Well, a witness is a person who sees what happens. It's his job to tell the truth, and give all the details of what took place, so that the police or the insurance company know whose fault an accident was. What he says is sometimes called his "testimony".'

'What's a false witness or a false testimony then, Dad?' asked Sarah, thinking of the commandment.

'To bear false witness or to give false testimony is to pretend to speak the truth but not really to do so,' explained her father. 'You see that motor-cyclist was really to blame. If I

75

said it was the fault of the driver of the car - perhaps, for example, because the motor-cyclist was my friend - I would be giving a false testimony. God's commandment tells me that I should always tell the truth and I should be especially careful to tell the truth when I'm talking about other people.'

Mrs MacDonald added, 'You know, people gave false testimony against the Lord Jesus.'

'When was that?' enquired Paul.

'The men who arrested the Lord Jesus took Him away to the high priest's house, where the chief priests, the elders and the doctors of the law were all waiting for Him. The chief priests and the whole council tried to find some evidence against the Lord Jesus, so that they could sentence Him to death. But they failed to find any. Lots of people gave false evidence against the Lord Jesus - that is, they said things about Him that weren't true at all. But their statements didn't agree. They weren't telling the truth.'

* * *

The park was full of people. There was so much to see. The flowers were blooming and the trees budding. They spent a little while watching the ducks and swans on the lake.

They watched horse-riders go past and the motor-boats on the lake.

'Here are a couple of questions for you,' said Mr MacDonald, thinking of something that would help the twins to understand the commandment a little more. 'How do those riders control their horses?'

'By the bits that are in the horses' mouths,' answered Paul.

'What about those boats? How are they directed?'

'By the tiny rudder at the back,' replied Sarah.

'Good,' said their father. 'A small bit in the mouth of a horse can control the whole horse. The tiny rudder at the back of a boat can direct its whole course. The tongue's like that. It's one of the smallest parts of your body, but it can do more good or more damage than any other part. A man who never says a wrong thing is a perfect man, and, of course, no one living on earth always controls his tongue properly. There's only one Person who has ever done that.'

'That was Jesus,' interrupted Sarah.

'That's right,' agreed Mr MacDonald. 'The Lord Jesus taught that we should be very

careful how we talk about other people. He said that sometimes we're better just saying yes or no in answer to people's questions, instead of saying a lot about other people.'

'Talking about this commandment,' said the twins' mother, 'reminds me of Uncle John.'

'Why, Mum?' asked Sarah.

'Dad and I can remember once when we were talking with Uncle John about one of our relatives and we weren't very kind in what we said. But we learned something from Uncle John. Every time we said something that wasn't very good about this person - even though it may have been true - he said something good.'

'Yes,' agreed Mr MacDonald. 'We learned a good lesson from Uncle John and you can too.'

10   Back to School

As soon as the twins had had their breakfast on Monday morning, they got their books ready for school. They pretended they were sorry to be going back after their time away. But, really, they were quite pleased. They had missed playing with their friends.

'I don't expect we'll have to do very much work today,' said Sarah, 'as it's the first day back.'

'No,' agreed Paul. 'We could take a book to read, couldn't we?'

'Have you thought of taking your Ten Commandments books to show Mrs Fox?' asked the twins' mother.

'No, and we don't want to show off,' said Sarah. 'And we haven't finished them yet; we still have the tenth commandment to talk about.'

'I wouldn't worry about that,' suggested Mrs MacDonald. 'Take them just in case there's an opportunity to show them to her. Knowing Mrs Fox as I do, I'm sure she'll be interested. Perhaps you could finish them tonight.'

Sarah and Paul took their books and set off

for school.

When the twins' class went into their classroom there was a tremendous noise and hubbub as everyone talked about what they had done on their holiday. When Mrs Fox came into the classroom she had difficulty in getting them quiet.

'Quiet now, children!' she cried out. 'I don't want to have to shout any more. After I've called the roll, instead of talking about your holiday, you can all write about it in your English exercise books!'

Paul and Sarah found this task quite easy. They wrote about their visit to the museum at the beginning of their holiday and all the things they had seen there.

After the midmorning break, Mrs Fox had time to talk to the children and to take up the usual lessons again.

'I'll be interested to read what you've written in your books,' she said. 'I'm sorry there was so much rain during the holiday. What did you do when it rained?'

Paul and Sarah looked at one another. They felt a little shy at putting up their hands about their Ten Commandments books, even though they had them with them. Philip put up

81

his hand first.

'Yes, Philip?'

'I played Monopoly with Keith. He came to my house twice when it rained.'

One after another the children put up their hands. 'What about you two - Paul and Sarah?' asked Mrs Fox. Paul and Sarah now had no alternative but to answer.

'We did a kind of project on the Ten Commandments some of the time, Mrs Fox.'

'That's interesting, Paul. How did you go about it?'

'Dad talked to us about the Ten Commandments, and he explained them to us. Then we had to write down in our own words what we thought the commandments meant and draw a picture or pictures to help us remember.'

'Have you brought them with you to school?'

Paul and Sarah produced their books from their desks.

'Why don't you pass them around the class?'

Sarah made a face. She wasn't too pleased that others would see her book, because the drawings weren't very well done. Then she thought of something. 'But I'm afraid we

haven't finished them yet. We still have the last commandment to do?'

'Oh well,' said Mrs Fox, 'we've a little while yet before the bell goes. We could talk about it. Does anyone know what the last commandment is?'

Paul and Sarah put up their hands. But Mrs Fox asked Angela White who put up her hand too. 'Yes, Angela?'

'We've been learning them at Sunday School, Mrs Fox. "You shall not covet" comes next. I forget the exact words but it tells us not to covet things that belong to other people.'

'Very good!' exclaimed Mrs Fox. 'What do you think "covet" means, then, Angela?'

Angela thought for a moment. 'Does it mean taking something that isn't yours?'

'No, that's stealing, isn't it? But it has something to do with what belongs to others.'

Andrew put up his hand. 'Is it wanting something that doesn't belong to you but belongs to someone else?'

'That's right,' agreed Mrs Fox. 'To covet is to want very much what someone else has. It usually begins with seeing something that someone else has and wishing that you had it. Sometimes we may find ourselves not liking someone else because he or she has something we wish we had.   Now I want you to be very honest, children.   Can you think of anything you've coveted?'

There was a pause for a moment. Suddenly Angela put up her hand.

'Yes, Angela.'

'I went to Sally's home on her birthday. She had lots of lovely birthday presents.   I told my mother that I wished I had some of the things that Sally has.'

Sally put up her hand then.   'I saw Nancy's new dress when she came to my birthday party. I felt angry that my mother hadn't been able to buy me a new one.   My mother said that perhaps Nancy's mother and father have more money than we have.   I said I wished we could change places and my father could earn more money.'

Mrs Fox smiled.   'Yes,' she said, 'those things all add up to coveting, like wanting to change places with someone, or feeling bad because someone has a dress or some sports equipment you want.   Coveting is like jealousy, isn't it?'

Paul had listened carefully and didn't quite understand.   So he put up his hand.

'Yes, Paul?'

'Is it wrong to want something then, Mrs Fox? I want a rucksack like Ralph's. On my birthday, Dad's going to buy me one.'

'No, that isn't wrong,' explained Mrs Fox. 'But it would be wrong if it were Ralph's rucksack that you wanted. God teaches us in this commandment that we're not to be worried all the time about things and about what other people have got which we haven't. Let me ask you all a question: Are you happy when you're jealous and covetous?'

No one answered.

'Let's put it another way. Are you happy when you're contented or when you're discontented?'

Paul put up his hand and answered. 'I think we're always unhappy when we're jealous.'

'I'm sure you're right,' agreed Mrs Fox. 'It's silly to covet. It's much better to learn to be content with what we have. If we become jealous of other people's possessions, we forget how much we have ourselves already and don't enjoy what we've got. God's law is an important secret for happiness. All right, children, write down in your own words what the commandment means and see what kind of picture you can draw to show its meaning. We'll see whose is the best.'

* * *

When Paul and Sarah arrived home, one of the first things they said to their mother was, 'We've finished our Ten Commandment books.'

'Finished them?   You still have number ten to do.'

'No! We did it in class.'

They then proceeded to tell her all that had happened at school.

'It wasn't such a bad idea after all to take your books was it?' commented their mother. 'Dad will be surprised. I do hope you've gained a lot from studying the commandments. Can you think of anything that you've especially learned?'

'I think the thing I've discovered,' said Sarah, 'is that no one keeps all the commandments and no one can.'

'That's certainly right.   God's commandments tell us God's will and they also show us how much we need the Lord Jesus as our Saviour.'

'But the Lord Jesus kept all the

commandments,' interrupted Paul.

'Yes,' said Mrs MacDonald. 'It was because of His obedience to them all that He could be our Saviour and die upon the cross, bearing the punishment for our disobedience to God's laws. God uses His laws to show us how much we need the Lord Jesus. When the Lord Jesus becomes our Saviour, and lives in us by His Holy Spirit, He helps us to keep God's laws.'

'We must keep our books on the commandments,' suggested Sarah.

'Yes, and most of all you must try to keep in your minds what you've learned about them,' added Mrs MacDonald.

Books

available from

Christian Focus Publications

Geanies House

Fearn, Ross-shire

write for our current catalogue

Bibletime Books

Carine Mackenzie

These are the stories of various Bible characters,
accurately retold from the Bible. These books are
lively and interesting and are combined with beauti-
fully illustrated pictures.

Old Testament Characters

Esther	- The Brave Queen
Gideon	- Soldier of God
Hannah	- The Mother who Prayed
Jonah	- The Runaway Preacher
Joshua	- The Brave Leader
Nehemiah	- Builder for God
Rebekah	- The Mother of Twins
Ruth	- The Harvest Girl

New Testament Characters

John	- The Baptist
Martha & Mary	- Friends of Jesus
Mary	- Mother of Jesus
Peter	- The Apostle
Peter	- The Fisherman
Simon Peter	- The Disciple

Learn About God

Carine Mackenzie

This series includes eight board books on the character of God for children of pre-school age.

Simple, easily read text is used throughout as well as delightful full colour illustrations.

God Has Power

God Answers Prayer

God Knows Everything

God Is King

God Is Faithful

God Is Everywhere

God Made Everything

God Never Changes

When The Rain Came

Eleanor Watkins

An exciting tale, centring around two boys and their developing friendship. Tom and his family hope to adopt Michael. The family are Christians and Tom has a conscience about his resentful behaviour towards Michael. The main excitement comes during a camping trip, when the boys find themselves left alone one night as the river floods. They attempt to save themselves and the equipment and Michael is almost swept away in the process. Finally, after being rescued they return to the farm where both boys have a sense of belonging; to each other, the family and God.

FULMAR SERIES - 7 to 10 years

The Coal-hole mystery

Teresa Crompton

A pleasant story set in an English village. The main characters are three girls - Amy Stewart (10), a newcomer to the village who becomes friendly with Lisa Ross (10); Sarah Corby (11) is a Christian and lives next door to Amy.

Sarah's and Amy's mothers become friends and they study the Bible together. A mysterious old character called Albert has a coal-hole which he keeps locked. Amy and Lisa are determined to find out what is in the coal-hole. By mischievous and devious means they break in and make an important discovery. Amy struggles with guilt because of the sad consequences of this. Sarah talks to her about Jesus and hleps Amy to explain things to her parents. The situation is resolved and Amy finally has the courage to tell LIsa their actions were wrong.

FULMAR SERIES - 7 to 10 years
ISBN 1 85792 209 3

Arabella Finds Out

Jacqueline Whitehead

Arabella, an oly child, comes from a very wealthy family. She is spoilt and finds it difficult to understand that not everyone is rich. Two village children befriend her, and begin to show her that possessions are not the only valuable things in life. Arabella persuades her paretns to let her go to the local school rather than a private one. She invites her class to her estate, hoping to impress them, but the trip results in a riot. This deepens her friendship with her two new friends and family. She comes to realise that God values a relationship with her and this is something that cannot be bought with money. Just as she begins to feel secure in her new friendships her father makes an announcement which turns the family's life around.

FULMAR SERIES - 7 to 10 years
ISBN 1 85792 161 5